Collected Poems

Ann Lax

Collected Poems

Collected Poems
ISBN 978 1 76109 146 9
Copyright © Ann Lax 2021

First published 2021 by
Ginninderra Press
PO Box 3461 Port Adelaide 5015 Australia
www.ginninderrapress.com.au

Contents

Dreamscape	7
Mornings	8
Winter	9
Drought	10
City v Country	11
Bush Insomnia	12
Generation Gap	13
Waiting Up	14
Keeping Up	15
Such is Life	16
Rummaging	17
Little Red Ridng Hood	18
Butterflies	19
One Lifestyle	20
In Our Element	21
The Elephant	22
The Actress	23
Stepford Wife	24
The Bowler	25
Denial	26
Human Nature	27
The Swallows	28
Busy Intersection	29
Challenges	30
Chocolate	31
The Way We Were	32
The Pianist	33
Autumn	34
Mrs So-and-so	35
Neighbour	36
On the Train	37

Dreamscape

She seeks sanctuary
in a world of dreams
solace from life's cares.
In this dreamlike state
shadows in the room
take on silhouettes
of long-forgotten ancestors
of aunts and uncles
from her childhood.
Snowflakes on the windowpane
generate dreams of white
cherry blossoms
drifting, drifting
like the snow outside.
Snow-covered trees
stand sculptured
as the fading evening light
draws to a close.

Mornings

It's autumn.
The patter of raindrops
can be heard
on the wattle leaves
outside my window.
I smell the rain.
When I try to stretch my limbs
the sheets enfold me.
I am a chrysalis.
My eyes open.
Dust motes dance
in the sunbeams
that filter through the blinds.
The clamour of the alarm clock
jars my early morning senses.
I step out of bed.

Winter

Nature slumbers.
Trees stretch naked limbs
skywards. But the heat is gone
and leaves litter the pavements.
The sun fades out early
and darkness makes its entrance
for an extended performance.
Cold-blooded creatures
withdraw to holes to await
the advent of spring.
Creeks that gurgled
between moss-covered banks
now stand still.
Ice draws tracery on windowpanes.
Frosts become the topic of the day.

Drought

The sun's baked the red earth
harder and harder
as far as eye can see.
Overhead a grey cloud swells
the colour of granite –
the promise of rain
tantalises
but doesn't eventuate.
Along the sun-cooked river bed
willows creak in the wind
wheel tracks and hoof prints
ghostly reminders
of a past life.

City v Country

He climbed the barbed wire fence
his face as stony as the granite
lying in the back paddock
you have a problem mate I said
it was as plain as the nose on my face
that he was as angry as a swarm of bees
don't mate me you peasant he said
having a shot at me won't
get you nowhere I said
just lay your cards on the table
upfront-like and we'll go from there
my BMW hit *your* roo he spluttered
and I've torn my Armani suit
on *your* fence
this bloke wants compensation
I thought my mind clicking
over like a cash register
we don't own the roos I said
and civilised people use the gate
you can leg it to the phone
just 30 kilometres down the road *mate*.

Bush Insomnia

A quiet day then shattered peace
as possums play tag
scamper across a tiled roof.
Weaned calves and indignant mothers
splinter the night air
with anguished bellows.
The bleating of a lost lamb
echoes down the valley.
6 a.m. Dawn creeps in like
a thief. A magpie's throaty
chorus celebrates morning.
A distant dog barks.
Day begins.

Generation Gap

I'm not sure when
I realised
you weren't perfect.

Maybe it was when
you placed a curfew
on my Saturday-night necking.

It might have been my first
dole cheque. You said I was
as useful as the hole in a donut.

Or when you found
my clothes too tight,
too short, too 'me'.

Or my body piercing made
you freak out like a sock
spinning in a dryer.

But you're still my mother.
A hundred years from now
we'll get it right. Maybe.

Waiting Up

She flits in and out of relationships
like a dragonfly skimming a pond

waiting up has kept me awake

I sit under the light bulb
a moth orbits my personal space
my presence does not disturb it

the night seems strangely silent
save the swish of cars along the road

I've left the radio on
humdrum noise to dull the night's vigil

there's a faint crackle in the corner
as a cockroach scuttles across cellophane

a key clicks in the lock
the front door swings wide
I stand up and brace myself.

Keeping Up

In our garden
We grow chokoes.
Our neighbours cultivate
Azaleas and rhododendrons.
They complain our vines are growing
Like Jack's Beanstalk
And invading their
(Dare I say it!)
Hallowed ground.

In their driveways
They have Volvos
With duco like satin.
In twenty years
Our battle-scarred Holden
(On blocks in the front yard)
Will be vintage.

In our street
Our neighbours prance
In and out of divorce
Like partners in a Scottish reel.
Their most venerable custom
Is the big mortgage.

In their front yards
For Sale signs sprout like dandelions.

Such is Life

Like the White Rabbit in *Alice*
I suffered from chronic lateness.
I managed to fix the tardiness
But caught a chill
Waiting for others to arrive.
I began attracting bugs
Like fish to a lure
Became a battleground for germs
Was as fragile as a sick spaniel.
'Lighten up,' the doctor said.
So I tried Laurel and Hardy
And split the sides of my jeans laughing
And threw out my shoulder.
The chiropractor was useful
But there was a very large charge.
It was the burning sensation
In my cheque account
That finally cured me.

Rummaging

I'm throwing out memories
of good intentions but lost causes.
Like the treadmill
I declared redundant –
prematurely I must add –
now at the back of the garage
unused since the Keating era.
My wardrobe bulges
like an overfed stomach
with clothes that never fit.
Brightly hued fungi
cultivated in tomato paste
for my young grandson – a scientist
of Florey proportions –
will have to go.
He's now a stamp collector
of great promise.

I'm trying to control
these bouts of optimism
and with an empty house
I can start all over again.

Little Red Riding Hood

Once Little Red Riding Hood
was jogging through Hyde Park
in a designer tracksuit with
a snazzy red hood and a basket
for Grandma crammed with goodies
from David Jones. She was new
to Sydney. Had never met
her granny. But not one to neglect
the oldies. Now Red Riding Hood
didn't know Granny had been
evicted for playing heavy metal rock
and entertaining street kids,
ne'er-do-wells and suchlike.
A 'granny' in drag was sitting
up in bed batting his eyelashes
like a venus flytrap.
Red Riding Hood noted the large eyes,
the large ears and the large false teeth
swimming in a glass
like some biological specimen
and still the cogs didn't
mesh. 'My dear, you are good
enough to eat.' Red Riding Hood,
a karate expert, trussed that old wolf
like a Xmas turkey in a trice.
She only paused to call
the police on her mobile.

Butterflies

My daughter and I
have been fighting for days.

We argue over what she wears,
what it costs and its absurdity.

She buys and I decry: stilettos
as lethal as their namesake.

Her designer model with tassels
dangling from the waist –

every playful feline for miles
will have fun with those.

Her butterfly brooch scrapes my ear.
Blood flows Chinese lacquer red

like her talons Her *pièce de resistance*
is a faux fur. Our dog thinking it

a large alsatian playing dead
whimpers and hides under the chair.

We no longer speak.
The silence unnerves.

But that butterfly looks good
on my new beige suit.

One Lifestyle

Forty-four years
She looks her age.
Her birthdays speed by
like the fugitive Harley
she rides pillion.
He thinks he's a god.
She's an accessory
like studs and leather
and machismo.
She hankers after suburbia.
He's in pursuit of thrills
as they ride through
one tired town after another.

In Our Element

My mother grows bonsai
in my lunchbox.
They thicken like gnarled ideas.
We play happy families
while my father the fireball
fumes at our hearth.
My parents try for understanding
but the syllables freeze on their lips.
They make love in glacial air
and their passion smoulders
like dry ice. I blow bubbles
with my little pipe to engender peace
but as they speak
their words catch fire
and the ashes float like minnows
under water across my feet.

The Elephant

Eight degrees centigrade at Taronga Park

Give her the smell
of decaying leaves
in a forest dripping green.
Ears attuned to the flap
of an owl's wing
as it glides darkly
through the night
are not in tune with
the whirligig
of autumn leaves
or the low moan of a winter wind.
Or the blaring of horns
the screech of tyres, polluting fumes
or pea soupers shrouding the harbour.
Without restraint let her wallow
in lagoons, roam grassy plains.

The Actress

She's at the crossroads
between youth and age
and can't accept the change –
like a hummingbird
beating the air with its wings
she flaps her hands in despair
rings, bracelets and necklace
in the footlights
a shimmering camouflage –
youth has passed like a heartbeat
age moves like a glacier
the burdens of fame are huge
and critics are everywhere
she remembers the early days
treading the boards as heroines.

What approval awaits her now
as she fades into old age?

Stepford Wife

She runs her house in the suburbs
with the efficiency of an automaton
the furniture glimmers from years of polish
like a cut diamond
she kisses her reflection
and leaves behind a cupid-bow mouth
her sheets flap on the line
like the sails of a cutter
she tracks down specks of dirt
with the frenzy of feeding fish
regards an invasion of ants
as a declaration of war
resents being told to remove
her shoes before entering
her daughter's cubby.

The dust settles on
the long-suffering silence
in the husband's shed.

The Bowler

My father was a bowler.
In the best tradition of bowlers
he was resplendent in white
in all weathers.
He grew young on the green
as though he'd sloughed
off his old self
but he never won a round
of anything but hard times.
It was only the very old like him
who had memories of the War,
the Depression
that clung to him like mistletoe
the legacy of his youth.
Drinks to hand,
in the pub scene afterwards
his chatter sounded on these themes
like a jammed horn.

Denial

She practises denial.
It's the flip side
to being a Pollyanna
as irritating as a buzzing fly.
She makes no mention
of birthdays
lets them swirl by
like a kite in the wind.
Youth grows old; their limbs wither
she remains young
to herself if no one else.

When she seeks perfection
like a painter plying his craft
she has a facelift
the transformation as temporary
as a passing cloud.
But friends move on, rejecting
wearing their age
like a badge of honour.
If there's an ache for old friends
that'll go. She'll just deny it.

Human Nature

Fifty years ago boys threw stones
now it's the clackety-clack
of computer keys or verbal ping-pong.
Insults? Cyber bullying?
(Tyranny by any other name)
Repute demolished brick by brick
like old buildings.
I listen while a male
holds his wine glass aloft
showing off his showmanship
swirls the shiraz
sniffs the aroma and swallows
then shreds the hostess's character
like an old file.

It's akin to the Cronulla riots
where youths hurled racial insults
like spears, each group spiking
the other, leaving a wreckage
of self-esteem – a clash that
boasts no victors.

I pause to think of those
who arrive in leaky boats.

The Swallows

When the house is still
and moonlight casts patchwork
shadows on the veranda
two swallows swoop and dive
swift as the thought of a passive observer
mindful of the straggly shreds of a new nest
and not wanting new paintwork
streaked with mud and straw
he swats with a broom.
Come morning light two swallows
roost on a wire and unblinking eyes
bear witness to their reproach.

Busy Intersection

On green
the crowd surges forward
a breaking wave
across the wet road
slick with rainbow oil.
Umbrellas jostle
black mushrooms
on the move.
A sudden gust plays havoc
sucking a few of them inside out
like a giant vacuum clean.

On green
cars zoom forward
like drivers in the
Mt Panorama circuit.
One clips the heels
of a recalcitrant pedestrian.
A windblown newspaper
flaps willy-nilly in the air
settles on a windscreen
like a huge moth.
The squeal of brakes
is followed by
the inevitable
crash of metal on metal.
Startlingly, the air is still with fear.

Challenges

My relationship with gadgets
is like flying a kite
on a calm day.
Tamper-proof bottles as puzzling
as a math equation languish
unopened in the pantry.
The remote control is a maze of
twists and turns.
Don't mention the mobile.
I race like a hare to answer
before they hang up
but quick as a raindrop
they are gone.
I am amazed at the steps
it takes to change the battery
in a pedometer.
It all seems mysterious
like wizardry.

Nothing has prepared me
for this brave new world.

Chocolate

Chocolate speaks
the language of love.
Its fragrance envelops
like a morning mist.
It took the English to turn
cocoa into a confection
more tempting than an apple.
Cocoa in Mayan culture
was the nectar of the gods
a symbol of life and fertility.
It's the Van Gogh of fruit trees
its pods – yellow originally – turn orange
exotic colours for an exotic fruit.
A fecund tree it uses a taller tree
as a sunshade.
Say what you will about chocolate
as a delicacy it's legendary.

The Way We Were

I breathed Mao
you lived reds under beds
and trod shopping malls
as if on safari.
We were incompatible
as far apart as the North and South Pole.

Your mind was confined
to thoughts of Tupperware.
It was the fire behind your eyes.
It lined your shelves
like toys in a toyshop
and edged out paperbacks
you said were a breeding ground for ideas.

Trying to connect, make meaning
our ideology at odds
and our voices raised like thunderclaps
we were exhausted, worn out, spent
and retreated into silence.

The Pianist

We are amazed at her skill
on the piano.

Each day she practises scales.
Her fingers move slowly
then grow nimble
as they trip up and down
like bees sipping flowers
for nectar. Her thoughts take flight
as she dreams of faraway places.
The steady tempo and rise
and fall of loudness
like a distant drum roll
weave patterns of sound
that calm us as her hands
brush the keys.

Skilfully, delicately,
she takes us into her world
of music.

Autumn

In her autumn years
and through the mists of time
she contemplates her childhood
her memories forming
a kaleidoscope of pattern
and colour and change.
Those years have flitted by
like doves on the wing.

She often lingers at sunset
when silence falls like a cloak
over the world
to glean knowledge from
these images of the past.

She closes her eyes
and the winds of rebirth
blow through her being.

Mrs So-and-so

Without raising her voice my daughter says
*I don't want to be seen with you. Your
clothes are too way-out. Calico and feathers
are not a good look.* Needless to say I make
my own clothes. She leaves Vogue designer
patterns around the house but I throw them
in the fire. She hides my needle. I have even
had to look for it in the cow barn. The whirr of
my sewing machine drives her into a frenzy.
Her foot-stamping has me in stitches. All
this has cast a web over our lives. She no
longer speaks. We are unravelling like
a spool of thread. The silence hems us in.

Neighbour

The man next door keeps revving
up his motor on the front lawn.
It has a music all its own, louder
than thunder, softer than footsteps.
A bass voice or a tuba practising
its range. My wife thinks it's a game
without rules, a game of one-upmanship.
His other neighbour owns a chainsaw.
Given the lack of distractions in this
neighbourhood, he is probably
creating a diversion. I would sell up,
but I like his style, and anyhow
the revving of his motor charts
the ups and downs of my life.

On the Train

On our train
you form a scrum
before you scrimmage
for a seat.
Once locomotion begins
static assembly lines
of black-suited robots
crackle papers
to punctuate their silence.
On our train
little men chant a mantra
'Tickets please'
and you are expected
to perform this sacred duty.
On our train
the most sporting custom
is the conga we dance
as we leave.
Hands on shoulders
with rhythmic roll
we spill into the subway
and are gone.

www.ingramcontent.com/pod-product-compliance
Lightning Source LLC
Chambersburg PA
CBHW062207100526
44589CB00014B/1994